MW00416661

DON'T LET
THE
STUFF
YOU LEAVE BEHIND
DESTROY
— YOUR —
FAMILY

Except where otherwise noted,
the opinions expressed in this book
are those of the author.

Revised 2nd Printing, January 2015

Copyright © 2014, Kenneth G. Hansen

Published by Praetorius Publishers

Distributed by Ringmasters
2437 N. Rulon White Blvd.
Ogden UT, 84404

To order additional copies of this booklet,
please visit www.RingmastersMedia.com.

ACKNOWLEDGEMENT

I would like to thank the following people for their help in preparing this booklet. I appreciate my wife, Kaye, for doing the original typing. The initial editing was done by my daughter-in-law Leslie Hansen. Christie Hansen, my niece, did additional editing and the final compilation.

CONTENTS

FOREWORD
Michael E. Bell

I first met Ken Hansen several years ago when we invited him to speak to a group of very seasoned financial advisors. Little did I know at the time that the simple concepts that Ken shared would prove to be invaluable to me and my family within a few short years. Unfortunately, my parents did not have an opportunity to read this little booklet, but the end result would have pleased them nonetheless. The concept of keeping families together after you pass is a very powerful and motivating idea that I know would have had my parent's full endorsement. I know that sounds obvious. Who doesn't want their families to get along and stay connected after the passing of their parents? Many are fairly good at making sure the legal documents are in place to take care of the "big stuff," but it is amazing how many families don't have a plan for the "stuff" that seems to cause the most hurt feelings and the negative emotions that can drive a wedge between family members.

There is a quote from Johann Kaspar Lavater in this booklet that says you don't really know a person until you have divided an inheritance with them. Growing up in a small community I knew of two siblings who would not talk to each other all because the wrong sibling got a particular piece of Dad's "stuff" when he died.

Again, at the time of Ken's presentation, I had no idea that the "perfect storm" was about to unfold for our family. I come from a blended family that came together after the loss of spouses--four children from my family and five from my stepfamily. After 30 years of marriage between my father and stepmother and shortly after Ken's presentation, my father passed unexpectedly at age 78. With wills and a trust in place and my stepmother being only 63 years old, there was no need to panic. We had time to talk about and mentally sort through "stuff."

When my stepmother died 3 years later, we all realized that even though the trust answered many questions, it didn't handle the "yours, mine, and ours" from a houseful of two lives of accumulation. From a car and baby grand piano on the "big stuff" side to a little trinket once displayed in a shadow box on the "small stuff" side. Everything seemed to have meaning to someone. Then there was the actual dollar value of artwork, collectible figures, and all that comes from years of travel and collecting.

What to do? Ken is always saying, "There are a hundred ways to skin a cat." Well, I would challenge you to find a better way than what you will find in this booklet. We followed Ken's advice down to every last detail. With a 30-yard dumpster for the junk and a truck and trailer for the goodwill donations in place, we started going through every item. Everyone had read the booklet and understood the ground rules. I was voted to be the auctioneer. I won't go into detail, but everyone walked away feeling like they received what was most important to them.

For some, due to circumstance and desire, they preferred to get money from the auction. For others, if something was important to them, they got it. You just don't know what is going to be important to someone else, even in your own family. The unexpected benefit of the whole experiences ended up being the opportunity we had to reminisce and hear funny stories about certain items. Because of the age difference in the siblings, many didn't know the history of some of the items and why an item may have special meaning to the family or a specific family member. There were some highly sought after things that seemed to get bid up well beyond their intrinsic value, but all of that gets worked out in the system. What could have been a nightmare ended up being a memorable and positive experience for everyone and allowed us to continue to build on these most important relationships with absolute transparency and understanding. This little booklet kept our family together. I don't believe there was another way to "skin this particular cat." Thanks Ken!

Hint—this booklet is best used and understood when parents are still alive and have embraced the concepts and everyone knows the wishes and expectations of a family that is going to stay united.

Mike graduated from Utah State University with a degree in finance. He also completed the Certified Financial Planning Program at The College for Financial Planning in Denver, CO. For the past 34 years Mike has owned and operated his own financial planning firm. He has worked with clients and advisors throughout the western United States. Lifelong friendships have developed from helping clients with their retirement and financial planning needs. Mike resides in Draper, Utah with his wife, Teresa. They have three married children and seven grandchidren.

Investment adviser representative offering securities and advisory services through Cetera Advisor Networks LLC, member FINRA/SIPC.
Cetera is under separate ownership from any other named entity.

PREFACE

Young Johnny journeyed with his family to visit their grandpa. Seeing Grandpa sitting in his Lane recliner, Johnny made a beeline for his lap. "Grandpa! Grandpa!" he said. "Make a noise like a frog."

"Why should I do that?" Grandpa asked.

"Because my mom says that as soon as you croak, we can take a trip to Disneyland."

If none of us ever croaked, there would be no need for this booklet and a lot less trips to Disneyland. However death, like taxes, is part of the cycle.

Can you face death knowing you have a program in place that is fair and honest and, if followed, will strengthen your family?

In a fun, short read this booklet will give you a road map to help you pass on your stuff – guns, the piano, Mom's rings and other personal items. The program outlined won't necessarily save your estate money, but it will save and strengthen your family. As my mom often said,

"Your most valued treasures are in your family photo album, not in your stock portfolio or real estate holdings."

Before I begin to outline how the auction estate settling process can strengthen your family, I must say that this booklet does not attempt in any way to take the place of a properly drawn will, trust, or partnership. I absolutely believe that every person should have at the very least a will, and possibly other professionally prepared legal documents such as trusts or partnerships. They should be drawn up by the best estate attorney you can find, so that you know you have done your best to preserve your hard-earned assets for your family, charities, schools, or church. You want to know that what you have worked for your whole life will go where you want it to go, and that it will be a blessing to those fortunate enough to receive of your efforts.

If you follow the outlined steps in this booklet, your family can be strengthened and your legacy will be assured.

CHAPTER ONE

Why are There Problems in Settling Estates?

"Experience keeps a dear school, but fools will learn in no other, and scarce in that, for it is true, we may give advice, but we cannot give conduct."
                                          –BENJAMIN FRANKLIN

In all my years in the investment business working with families of deceased parents, I must say that I do not recall any children being critical of their mom or dad because of their lack of success in their overall investment program. They aren't concerned with the size of their parents' estate. They accept things as they are. Where the problems come forth is the way the estate is divided and whether or not it is fair.

Children, no matter what the age, want to feel loved by their parents. They want to feel they were loved as much as their brothers and sisters. They want to know favoritism was not part of the equation.

Let me illustrate with this story. When my mom died, Dad was retired from a very successful career as a dairy farmer. He owned a good portfolio of stocks, bonds, and partnerships and, of course, the dairy farm with all the cattle and equipment to make the operation go. The farming operation was where the bulk of the assets were. There were two girls and four boys in our family – all married and successful. We were all together at Dad's place. Dad said, "I have been really blessed. I have more than I need. How do you feel and what are your thoughts on how I should divide up the things I have accumulated in a lifetime?"

Two of my brothers were farmers and there was some concern that they would get the farm where 80 percent of the estate's value was, not leaving much to the other four children. Connie, my sister, made a statement I will never forget. She said, "Dad, this is your place. You have worked hard for it. I would be happy if you spent every dollar, and if you ever needed help I would help you. But when you die, I would hope that if you have assets left, that you would be fair and equal to all of the children."

Connie was married to a successful health physicist and had a lovely home and family. What she really was saying was, "Dad, the money isn't important, but your love is. I hope that my brothers and sisters are all loved equally. If the estate (whatever it is) is shared equally, we will be happy with you and with each other."

I absolutely believe that if parents want their children to be close and remain close, they must be fair and equal with each one.

Are there any exceptions to the rule? Absolutely! I can think of many family situations where special plans need to be made to accommodate certain needs and requirements. For examples, one or more of the children may still be minors. One child may have health issues or other special needs. This could extend to grandchildren as well. I'm sure you can think of many more examples. In any event, these situations need to be dealt with properly by using legal documents such as wills and trusts. During this process, all of the children should be involved and be part of the solutions. Only when children fully understand the decisions, the whys and why nots, can there be unity.

It is not the big things that seem to cause the hurt and frustration among siblings. The big things are straight-forward. If there are stocks, you simply take the number of shares of each company and divide them by the number of children. If there is a home or car involved, they can be sold, and then the money is split evenly. Most problems arise over the personal effects – the small stuff. Hence, the need for this booklet.

CHAPTER TWO

Stories and Problems

"It's true that you can't take it with you. But folks ought to remember that how you got it may determine where you go." – AUTHOR UNKNOWN

We all know someone or have heard of an example where dividing an estate has created some problems within a family. Full disclosure is vitally important in the division of a family estate. For example, if one child has borrowed money, when will it be paid back? Will it be deducted from their share of the estate? Will interest be paid?

In this chapter I am going to share some stories that will show why I feel this booklet's approach to dividing personal effects is needful. These stories may help you avoid some of the pitfalls you could encounter. Some of my stories or examples may have religious overtones. Please don't get caught up in the religious references. Just try to get a vision of the problems created. The events are true. I am going to change the names except in my own family and hope not to embarrass anyone.

Before we get into the stories I will repeat what Dear Abby quoted from Johann Kaspar Lavater, "Say not that you know another entirely till you have divided an inheritance with him."

Story One

Some years ago a widow of thirteen years passed away, leaving her children and thirteen grandchildren. My sister, president of the women's organization of her church, went to visit one of the daughters who had lived closest to the deceased. My sister offered her condolences and, as was the custom, offered to provide a luncheon for the family after the funeral services.

The daughter's response was, "Don't bother! I don't want to be in the same room with those greedy people. I can't stand the hypocrites."

It seems that this daughter, the one that lived closest, helped her mom clean, ran her to the store, church, doctor and pharmacy. She had spent countless hours and gas serving her mother's needs for many years. The other three siblings, who lived a little further away, but in the same city, never lifted a finger to help. Oh, they called on Mom's birthday and stopped by on Christmas, but not much more.

One day, a year or so before the mother's death, a grandson belonging to one of the non-attentive families started dropping by to visit Grandma. She appreciated his visits very much. One day he explained that most of her grandchildren had homes and were doing well. He explained that he would like to buy her home. Of course she was not interested as she loved her home and wanted to live there until she died. He explained how that was not a problem. She could live in the home until her death and then, and only then, would the deal go through.

She thought that would be okay. She explained how she and Grandpa had built the home twenty years earlier at a cost of about $80,000. The grandson said that $80,000 would be a fair price, and he would be happy to pay that. After some thought, the grandma agreed. They decided that 5 ½ percent would be an acceptable rate on a 30-year loan.

Grandpa and Grandma had spent their whole life working and serving others by doing genealogy work and trying to put families together. Grandma had continued in that work for thirteen years since Grandpa's death.

All of the children knew that the only thing Grandma owned of any real value was her home, and that the value of the home had gone up considerably. They expected the home to be sold at her death, when each of the children would receive ¼ of the home's value (the home was appraised at about $200,000).

Because of the grandson's contract with Grandma, instead of each of her children receiving $50,000 plus in cash, it turned out that they received $20,000 over a 30-year period plus 5 ½ percent interest. Needless to say, there was much anger and frustration when they found out the grandson had bought the home without the family knowing.

A mom who worked her whole life to put families together, through one bad decision, ended up destroying her own family. If Grandma had just called her family together and discussed the sale of her home with them, all of the hurt and frustration could have been avoided.

Story Two

Melvin, one of seven children, tells about when his mom died. His dad had already passed away two years earlier. The family all met at the mom's apartment in the southern part of the state. Melvin and family planned to go to the viewing, funeral and cemetery. Afterward, the family planned to return to mom's apartment and divide up the mother's things. A sister from California said that she had a bad headache and wanted to lie down and would catch up with them later.

She never showed! It seems she drove from California with a moving truck and parked it a block away. When the family came back to Mom's apartment, it had been cleaned out and the sister and U-haul were long gone. Just imagine the fun family reunion they had that summer.

Story Three

Mary was an accomplished pianist and had one sister who didn't play at all. Their parents owned a beautiful baby grand piano. Mary was told that because she played and loved music so much, the piano was to be hers when the parents passed away.

Dad passed away first and then Mom. It was now time to divide their property. They decided to sell the home and divide the proceeds. A month after the home was listed, Mary decided to drop by the house. What a shock! The piano was gone. An investigation was made. Yes, the sister who didn't play had taken the piano. Yes, there were words and feelings. Relations were strained. What could have been a beautiful relationship with sisters and cousins was not to be.

Story Four

Ned was one of six children in a wonderful, warm and close family. The parents were kind and giving in word and deed. When Dad died, Mom wanted to get rid of his things. He had horses, equipment, four wheelers and more.

Ned came to me one day saying, "I need help. What should I do? Mom wants me to handle the division of the property since I am the oldest. Dad was the most giving person I have ever known. Everything my dad owned he promised or gave away at least three or four times."

I asked him what the problem was. He said, "The problem is with the kids. Whenever Dad promised something to Steve, my younger brother, Steve would thank him and say, 'So we don't forget, I'll write this up on a piece of paper and you sign it. Then there will be no misunderstanding.'"

At a family meeting where they planned to divide everything, Steve brought out all of his signed papers. Lo and behold, he owns everything. The air became thick with hurt feelings.

Ned said, "I felt like I had been tied down onto a railroad track. I couldn't move, and I could hear the train coming."

Story Five

Talking with a friend the other day, I asked him how he was going to divide his estate. "Well," he said, "We are already telling the kids what we are going to leave them."

I asked him if his children were happy with the decisions that were made. He replied, "No, they are not. For example, I told my oldest son he would get his great-grandfather's railroad watch and chain. Our second son plays the piano. We told him he would have our grand piano. Our first son's wife spoke up and said, 'That isn't fair. An old watch compared to a grand piano?' The meeting got hot after that, so we stopped there."

My friend said he thought he and his wife would divide things up the way they wanted to, and later on the kids could worry about it after Mom and Dad were gone. Here again, fairness became the issue.

Story Six

I was talking with a client on the phone. I asked Al if he had his estate set up the way he wanted it to be. "No, I don't. I am just now trying to get my mom, a widow, to get her things in order. She doesn't have much, so I'm not concerned about getting anything. My sister and brother can have it all. I don't care."

"Okay," I said. "So, if your mom died tomorrow and had a will which said, 'I leave everything I have equally to Tom and Alice and nothing to Al,' you would feel fine about it?"

"Well," he said, "as I think about it a little more, maybe I would not feel too good about it."

Al makes a great point. Even though he has been very successful in life and doesn't lack for anything material, what he is saying is "I would like to feel that Mom loves me equally with my sister and brother." She has tried to be fair.

Story Seven

Not long ago four people came into my office. There were two sisters and two brothers. Their dad had died two years previously, and their mother had passed away just a month ago.

As they came in I could feel tension in the room. I went over their mom's legal paper and told them we would do as the papers directed – transfer one quarter of their mom's account to each of them individually.

They all left.

In about fifteen minutes the two brothers came back and said, "We want to talk to you alone." They explained that when their dad was alive, he tried to be fair. But after his death, their mom showed a great deal of favoritism to their sisters. She would give them money and many other things. They didn't feel, at this point, that getting one quarter interest in what was left was fair. They wanted to know what I could do to make it more equal.

I could do nothing other than follow the legal documents. They left with feelings not of gratitude for what was left to them, but of bitterness against their mom and sisters. They did not feel that they had been treated fairly.

Story Eight

A friend of mine is a funeral director. He told me that they have to own more than one limousine because many times there is so much contention between family members that they will not ride in the same vehicle to the cemetery.

Story Nine

Remember when your children were toddlers, you gave each a cookie or dish of ice cream? Their eyes would look at their own, then at their brother's and sister's portions, and if they were not exactly the same, "How come they got more than me?" Even then, fairness was an issue. So whether five, twenty-five or fifty-five, fairness is a concern among siblings.

In summary, fairness, disclosure and communication come to the forefront. I have recited a few stories and could tell many more, but the end result is always the same. Parents are not fair with their children if they do not disclose their plans and communicate them in an open way so that all feel good about things. If that communication doesn't take place, there can be pain, hurt, frustration, and misunderstandings that can last a lifetime.

I know that each of you could tell your own stories about neighbors, friends and your own relatives who have had challenges settling estates. As you think about your own experiences or the ones I have related, disclosure, communication and fairness must always be the keystone principles.

Chapter Three

Using a Family Auction to Divide Estate Assets

"If a new, married couple will live the first ten years of their married life like few people will, they can live the rest of their life like few people can."

- JOHN TEMPLETON

There are several ways to settle an estate. I am assuming at this point that the will, trust, etc. are in place. I am going to present a plan that will work to divide the small stuff. It is fair, honest, and if followed will keep the family united and together. The beauty of this plan is its simplicity. There will be questions, and in this chapter I will do my best to answer them.

The Family Auction

The last parent has died. What is next? Follow this plan and I promise some good things will happen.

Set a date, a month out if possible when all the family can be present. This will give bidders time to think about the stuff so the sentimental value can be factored in.

One lady told me that in their family auction the washer and dryer (both in excellent condition), went for $20.00, but their fathers' old fishing hat went for $300.00.

Plan the whole day together. Have the auction start around 9:00 a.m. Have food ordered for lunch. We had pizza and root beer. Appoint an auctioneer. This can be any of the children of the deceased, and that person can bid also. The children can decide if spouses and/or grandchildren can attend and bid.

An auctioneer and secretary should be appointed to record items bought, who bought them and the amount of the highest bid. The auctioneer and secretary can also bid on items.

Let family members go into the home before the auction starts and look over the items that will be auctioned. Nothing is to be taken from the premises prior to the auction except for perishables.

My mother died fifteen years before Dad. Dad died on January 4th, and the auction date was set for February 15th at 9 o'clock. I was the oldest of the six children and was appointed auctioneer.

My sister came to me as she was looking over Dad's things and said, "I gave Dad a beautiful quilt for Christmas, and it was never used. I would like it back."

"Wait a minute," I said. "You said you gave it to

Dad for Christmas."

"Yes I did," she replied.

"Well then, it is his like everything else that has been given by you or the other children, or he has bought. So if you would like it back, you be the high bidder and it is yours." She understood and was satisfied with my answer.

A one-month notice of the auction date is important. It gives the family a little time to think about things and talk with their spouses about which items hold the most sentimental value for them.

If there are no bids or interest in an item, put that item in a special place where it can later be given to a charitable organization. You can choose the charitable organization by a majority vote of the children.

During our auction we found twelve silver dollars hidden in a drawer. None of them had great value, so I put them in a box and had each of the six children draw out two. If there had been fifteen I would have had everyone draw out two and auction the rest to the highest bidder.

I use the situation of the silver dollars to illustrate that if something out of the ordinary pops up, a little common sense can keep everything smooth, fair, honest, and above the table.

At the start of our family auction I sensed a little heartburn and anxiety among the group. But as everyone saw what was going on and the total fairness of the event, the anxiety melted away and everyone felt fine. I felt an increased appreciation for our parents and each other as brothers and sisters.

At the end of the day we had sold close to $50,000 worth of stuff – a GMC pickup truck, a Thunderbird car, twenty-four yearling heifers, farm equipment, household furniture and all the things a family accumulates over a lifetime. This amount didn't include the home that was sold later, or the stocks, bonds and CDs that had been divided equally a couple of weeks before the auction.

When we got to Dad's clothes closet, there were two almost new suits which had cost Dad over $350 each. The bidding started, got up to $15 and then stopped! John had the highest bid. He was the only one of the six sons and sons-in-law who could get into the suits. I said, "Give us $15 for the second suit." He said, "No. Twelve dollars is tops." No one else would bid higher.

If you are the right size, you may get an even better deal at your family auction.

Chapter Four

Dividing Proceeds at the End
of the Family Auction

"I have found the best way to give advice to your children is to find out what they want, and then advise them to do it." – HARRY S. TRUMAN

In this chapter I want to talk about dividing the proceeds of the auction.

At the conclusion of the auction, have a calculator and add up each person's items that they were the high bidder on, so that each person knows the total amount that they owe for the things they bought.

Then take the lowest total from each of the children's total. The amount left after that deduction is made is the amount owed by that person to the family. For example, let's say that five siblings have totals as follows:

Marsha	$12,000
Harry	$11,000
Beth	$10,000
Stuart	$9,000
Anne	$8,000

Anne has the lowest total at $8,000. That amount would be subtracted from each of the children's totals. The remaining amounts would be:

Marsha	$4,000
Harry	$3,000
Beth	$2,000
Stuart	$1,000
Anne	-0-

Each person then writes out a check for the amount they owe the family.

Next, add up the check amounts to get a grand total. Divide this grand total by the number of children in the family. This figure is the amount that each child is due back to them as their fair share.

Using the numbers from the above example, the

grand total for our example family would be $10,000. This number would be divided by 5, the number of children in this family. The result is $2,000. This is the amount that each child gets back as their share of the proceeds.

Either before or during the auction, everyone had a chance to see what they were bidding on. If they were the highest bidder, they own it. If they bought a lamp or a vase and find it has a crack in the base, they own it crack and all. You do not turn anything back in or try to renegotiate the price. High bid owns it.

Likewise, if you buy a picture as the high bidder and later find a $100 bill taped to the back, you own the picture plus the bill. Also, you own it if you find the picture is appraised for a great deal of money.

Everything is auctioned "as is." If it is broken after bidding, then whoever bought it owns something that is broken. In our auction we had a pickup load of things going to charity, and another pile going to the dump. There were a couple of items that people bought and later decided they didn't want. Those items went in the charity pile, and no, they did not get any money back.

Chapter Five

Perceived Problems to Holding a Family Auction

"Money is a good servant but a bad master."
– FRENCH PROVERB

Of all the chapters in this booklet, this is the hardest to understand because of preconceived notions. The auction concept is very simple and straightforward. It is totally fair and keeps everyone honest.

Because of habits, education, birth or marriage there is usually a wide margin in the wealth status of different children in a family. In the past when I have talked about estates using the auction concept, the first reaction is usually negative. Why? Most everyone has heard of or been to an auction. The negative reaction is usually because people really don't understand the principle. I will try to explain the common objections.

My father-in-law had passed away some years ago. When I mentioned the auction concept to my mother-in-law, this was her reaction – "It sounds okay for some families, but it won't work for ours." I asked her why not. She said, "Well, two are well off and three have no extra money. So the ones with the money can come in and buy up everything and leave the three others with nothing but hard feelings."

Wrong. Wrong. Wrong!

In the first place, the rich ones probably already have most of their needs and wants fulfilled. They will bid on much less than you think.

My mother-in-law did not want an auction. She went around the home and put names on many objects which the girls had commented they would like to have. Years and years passed by. The girls went home to divide things up after their mother's funeral. At this point they didn't need or want many of the things that they had their names on, but some of the grandchildren were interested in some of the items.

If a child only bids on their percentage of the personal items, it will cost them zero. Not one red cent. Why? Because at the close of bidding, every dime is accounted for then added up and immediately given back to the siblings based on the number of children in the family. If one child wants more than their share or percentage, then and only then will they need to reach into their own pocket. And even then I submit that they will get what they buy at a bargain basement price.

Let's re-use the family mentioned in chapter four to

illustrate.

Siblings	High Bids	Minus Low	Adjusted Total
Marsha	$12,000	-$8,000	$4,000
Harry	11,000	-8,000	3,000
Beth	10,000	-8,000	2,000
Stuart	9,000	-8,000	1,000
Anne	8,000	-8,000	0

When all of the adjusted totals were tallied, the grand total was $10,000. When the grand total is divided by the number of children in this family (5), everyone's fair share is $2,000. Looking at the layout below, you can see that Marsha and Harry were the only ones who actually paid anything out-of-pocket.

Siblings	owed to family	fair share	final
Marsha	$ <4,000>	+ 2,000	$2,000 owed to family
Harry	<3,000>	+ 2,000	1,000 owed to family
Beth	<2,000>	+ 2,000	-0-
Stuart	<1,000>	+ 2,000	1,000 Received from family
Anne	-0-	+ 2,000	2,000 Received from family

For every dollar spent in a family estate auction, each siblings share will come back to them. For example: if there are four children, each child will receive 25% back from every dollar they spend bidding on items. If one child doesn't want to bid on any of the items and the others do, then that child will take home cash. That cash will be equal to their share of the total value of the personal items based on the bidding of the rest of the siblings.

At the end of the auction each person has had a full opportunity to bid or not to bid. If they didn't get what they wanted, it was because they didn't want it badly enough to be the high bidder. There should not be any hard feelings against any sibling.

My dad kept my mom's engagement and wedding rings. I thought for sure that his oldest daughter would be the high bidder for them, but she wasn't. She dropped out of the bidding early on. But my youngest brother and sister wanted them big time. Bidding went up to their value and then higher and higher. The bids were higher than their price at the jewelry store in town. Finally my sister said, "I would like them, but at that price I would rather have the cash." She let my younger brother have them. He said, "Great! I am glad I got them, but I wish you had stopped bidding sooner." Everyone laughed and was happy the way it had worked out.

Chapter Six

Involving Grandchildren in the Auction

If you would like, invite your grandchildren to attend the family auction. In our family, we plan to have grandchildren attend. Our reasoning is, our children all have homes and if they have a bedroom it already has a bed, etc. Some of the grandchildren may need or want some of the stuff that would not be of interest to their parents. Yes, the parents may have to store their stuff for a while.

Next big question, where do grandkids get money to bid? Most of them do not have a lot of money and may need some help from parents. Also, parents can help their children in bidding on things they want.

In my family we have a family partnership, owned by our children and grandchildren. My wife and I directed that upon my death (my wife died in Jan. 2014), each grandchild will be given $2,000.00 from the partnership and will be invited to the auction. They can take the money and "go south" or can spend any or all at the auction. What they don't spend, they keep. I'm sure they will get some great buys. Of course, what they spend goes right back into the partnership which is owned by the kids and grandkids.

Another family, after the death of the grandparents, the children would fund the grandchildren's purchases. So there are a number of ways to have the grandchildren involved. Just think it through and make sure your plan is totally fair and honest for each of them.

Another family with eight children (plus eight spouses) and forty-seven grandchildren didn't have room in the home for everyone to attend the auction. So they video-taped the contents of each room and each family viewed the video. This way the grandchildren can tell their parents what they have an interest in and the parents can represent them at the auction. The parents then bid on what the family wants, and the family settles the money issues within the family. Remember if the family bids on their share, it costs them nothing.

Chapter Seven

Preserving Traditions and Family Values

"Family faces are magic mirrors. Looking at people who belong to us, we see the past, present and future. We make discoveries about ourselves. – GAIL LUMET BUCKLEY

This could be the most important chapter you will read. Its principles and ideas will be felt not for months, but for years.

Dad owned a real estate contract that was a second mortgage on a home where the buyer was also behind on the first mortgage. The payments had stopped some months before. Yes, we could foreclose, but I didn't think the contract had much, if any, value. The auction was about over. As we discussed the contract and its worth and what we might want to bid, I said, "Let's not sell the contract. Let me manage it. I'll collect what I can and put it into a 'Hansen Party and Reunion Fund.'" Everyone agreed!

I wrote a few letters and gave the buyer a full accounting, so that they would know that even though

Dad was gone, we still expected payment. Wouldn't you know, every once in a while a payment would come in. Then one day I received a call. The buyer told me that she had received some money and if I would discount the note, she would send me $5,000. The deal was agreed to, and we now have over $8,000 in the fund.

If my dad and mom could know of all the things we have done with the money we got from that contract, they would be very pleased. Why? This fund has paid for and provided more parties, dinners, reunions, presents, and get-togethers than I can count.

As I said in the beginning of this booklet, the whole purpose of conducting an auction is to keep peace in the land by keeping families together and keeping them talking and having fun together. I have seen only good come out of doing things together.

As my children and grandchildren associate with their cousins, some interesting things happen. They see cousins excelling on the piano, in school, church activities, scouting, and work. All of a sudden things that were not cool before now become cool. All of my brothers and sisters seem to go out of their way to build up and strengthen nieces and nephews to do better and stand a little taller.

I could go on and on, but let me sum up with a very important statement. When you get involved with your parents' estate, or when planning your own, try to make provisions for a fund like the one described in this chapter. Put your heads together, use your imaginations and do some brain-storming. Come up with some ideas for family get-togethers and start doing things that will build and strengthen family traditions. This may take a little work, so pass the responsibility around.

Good luck! The dividends will be many and far-reaching. Remember, if you're only planning for a year, plant wheat. If you are planning for 50 years, plant a tree. If you are planning for generations as far as you can see, plant traditions and values in the heart of a boy or a girl.

Chapter Eight

Summary

"A poor man will walk a mile to save a dollar. A rich man will walk five miles to save a dollar."

– AUTHOR UNKOWN
(favorite quote of my father, Glen H. Hansen)

In summary, I would like to share just a few closing thoughts. We are living in very troubled times. We all need to give and receive support from each other. A little encouragement and a bit of compromise can be a great blessing to all of us.

In Acts 10:34 Peter said, "Of a truth I perceive that God is no respecter of persons." In other words, God loves all of his children equally and doesn't respect one over another. So, each of us in that same spirit should try to do the best we can at being totally fair and honest with our own children. If we are not, or if it is perceived that we are not equal and fair, hurt and strained relationships can develop. These can cause splits and breakups of brothers and sisters that were once close and loving.

Now you have read this booklet. You think the

auction program will work in your family. You are committed to the concepts of fairness and honesty. Proceed by having each family member read this and then call a family meeting and agree on the rules and guidelines as I explained in Chapter Three.

Finally, go to chapter six and lay out a plan for future family parties and reunions. How much do you want in the fund? Who will be in charge the first year? Decide what, where and when for the events of that first year.

Remember, parents never outlive their responsibility to their children.

PHILOSOPHY OF INVESTING AND SAVING

Your savings and investments, believe it or not, affect the way you stand, the way you walk, the tone of your voice; in short, your physical well-being and self-confidence. People without savings and investments are always running. They must. They must take the first job offered, or nearly so. They sit nervously on life's chairs because any small emergency throws them into the hands of others.

Without investments and savings people must be grateful. Gratitude is a fine thing in its place, but a constant state of gratitude is a horrible place in which to live. People with savings and investments can walk tall. They may appraise opportunities in a relaxed way, have time for judicious estimates and not be rushed by economic necessity.

People with savings and investments can afford to resign from their job if their principles so dictate. And for this reason they will never need to do so. Those who can afford to quit are much more useful to their company, and therefore more promotable. They can afford to give their company the benefit of their most candid judgments.

People always concerned about necessities such as food and rent can't afford to think in long-range career terms.

People with savings and investments can afford the wonderful privilege of being generous in family or neighborhood emergencies. They can take a level stare from the eyes of anyone, friend, stranger, or enemy. It shapes their personality and their character.

The ability to save and invest has nothing to do with the size of income. Many people with high incomes spend it all and are on a treadmill, darting through life like minnows.

The dean of American bankers, J. P. Morgan, once advised a young broker: "Take waste out of your spending, and you'll drive the haste out of your life."

If you don't need money for college, a home or retirement, then save for self-confidence. The state of your savings and investment program does have a lot to do with how tall you walk.

ABOUT THE AUTHOR

Ken grew up on a dairy farm in Cache Valley, Utah. He graduated from Utah State University in Economics and Finance and also studied at Wharton School of Business. He has been a financial consultant for over 50 years. He has twice been a branch manager of brokerage firms, has been involved in owning and developing several shopping centers and housing developments, and has taught many seminars at universities, church and civic groups in Utah and Idaho. He has also operated cattle ranches in Utah, Nevada, and Wyoming. He is a father of five children and has twenty-three grandchildren.

Ken has served in a number of different positions in leadership and humanitarian positions in his church. Ken has lived in Bountiful, Utah for 50 years. His greatest love is helping people (friends) accomplish their financial goals. He believes, like Mark Twain, "that though you have a thousand friends, you have not one to spare."

Personal Recommendations:

Dear Mr. Hansen,

I read your booklet shortly after my father passed away. As suggested in the booklet, we held an auction for the household and personal property. Your ideas worked very well for us, as we found the distribution of goods a pleasant time, full of reminiscences and apprectiation. The stress of worrying about who received any particular item was removed by the opportunity each person had to bid for anything he/she might want. There was a great feeling among family members and no contention. Thank you for sharing a great idea.

Sincerely,

Elyse Harris

Dear Ken -

Your approach to settling estates offers a simple solution to a profoundly difficult family problem. I am amazed more has not been written on the subject. Your book is so convincing, I'm enclosing a check for five more copies to share with family and friends.

Thank you for sharing your wisdom on this important subject.

Best Personal Regards,

Steven P. Houghton

This book has some excellent ideas that could benefit many families.

Orrin Hatch, U.S. Senator

This book gives many of us a fascinating solution for a potentially sticky problem.

Elaine Hatch

CPSIA information can be obtained at www.ICGtesting.com
Printed in the USA
BVOW04s1446090415

395395BV00003B/6/P